JALOUSIE

PREVIOUS WINNERS OF THE BERKSHIRE PRIZE
Tupelo Press First / Second Book Award

Xiao Yue Shan, *then telling be the antidote*
Selected by Victoria Chang

Brandon Rushton,
The Air in the Air Behind It
Selected by Bin Ramke

Iliana Rocha, *The Many Deaths
of Inocencio Rodriguez*
Selected by Oliver de la Paz

Laurel Nakanishi, *Ashore*
Selected by Carl Phillips

Anna Marie Hong, *Fablesque*
Selected by Aimee Nezhukumatathil

Elizabeth Acevedo,
Medusa Reads La Negra's Palm
Selected by Gabrielle Calvocoressi

Patrick Coleman, *Fire Season*
Selected by Carol Frost

Jenny Molberg, *Marvels of the Invisible*
Selected by Jeffrey Harrison

Amy McCann, *Yes, Thorn*
Selected by Paisley Rekdal

Kristina Jipson, *Halve*
Selected by Dan Beachy Quick

Ye Chun, *Lantern Puzzle*
Selected by D.A. Powell

Mary Molinary,
Mary & the Giant Mechanism
Selected by Carol Ann Davis and
Jeffrey Levine

Daniel Khalastchi, *Manoleria*
Selected by Carol Ann Davis and
Jeffrey Levine

Megan Snyder-Camp,
The Forest of Sure Things
Selected by Carol Ann Davis and
Jeffrey Levine

Jennifer Militello, *Flinch of Song*
Selected by Carol Ann Davis and
Jeffrey Levine

Kristin Bock, *Cloisters*
Selected by David St. John

Dwaine Rieves, *When the Eye Forms*
Selected by Carolyn Forché

Lilias Bever, *Bellini in Istanbul*
Selected by Michael Collier

David Petruzelli,
Everyone Coming Toward You
Selected by Campbell McGrath

Bill Van Every, *Devoted Creatures*
Selected by Thomas Lux

Aimee Nezhukumatathil,
Miracle Fruit
Selected by Gregory Orr

Jennifer Michael Hecht,
The Next Ancient World
Selected by Janet Holmes

Winner of the Berkshire Prize

The title of this stunning collection refers to a window treatment which has rows of angled slats, like blinds or shutters, and Allyson Paty's disarming lyric exemplifies a deliciously sharp perspective which at times ranges from being seen literally through partially-opened slats, the world at a slant, to confronting the mediations of how we tender our communications, representations of self, labor, and love. These are poems reminiscent of the cutting lines of Elaine Kahn and Elisa Gabbert, but these poems are uniquely their own.

Here, where "vision began / and ended was *medias res*," *Jalousie* may feel like mid-stream meditations but are in fact wholistic wrestlings with what it means to live and work in today's metropolis: subjects tackled are: technology (phones, computers), capitalism, being an object of the state, but also the leisure of "watching *Blow Up*" on the sofa with "Krasdale Puffed Rice with Real Cocoa" in hand. At its core, these poems explore "the condition of place / inside a body," the body within an urban place, and also the body cognizant of contextual history.

The speaker of the poem "In Medias Res," knows to "shut [their] eyes / to receive," which is to say, to listen to one's surroundings in order to catch details the eye often misses. Allyson Paty understands that "*to see / is to have at a distance //* what populates vision" and the "distance" in their case is a view filtered as if through shutters—hidden, protected—but because there is "not quite so much sun," is able to receive much more of scene. And by the final line in this fine collection, the poet shares what we've been privy to all along, that is, that they do, quite radiantly, "resolve the view, unstriped and entire."

—from the Judge's Citation by Diana Khoi Nguyen

JALOUSIE Allyson Paty

TUPELO PRESS T|P North Adams, Massachusetts

First edition April 2025.

ISBN-13: 978-1-961209-21-3 (paperback)
Library of Congress Control Number: 2024948363

Library of Congress Cataloging-in-publication data available on request.

Cover and text design by Ann Aspell

Cover art: Erica Baum, *Aquas Paleatus (Naked Eye Natural World)*, 2018, archival pigment print, 18 × 16 in. Courtesy of the artist and Bureau, New York.

Tupelo Press
P.O. Box 1767
North Adams, Massachusetts 01247
(413) 664-9611 / Fax: (413) 664-9711
editor@tupelopress.org / www.tupelopress.org

Tupelo Press is an award-winning independent literary press that publishes fine fiction, non-fiction, and poetry in books that are a joy to hold as well as read. Tupelo Press is a registered 501(c)(3) non-profit organization, and we rely on public support to carry out our mission of publishing extraordinary work that may be outside the realm of the large commercial publishers. Financial donations are welcome and are tax deductible.

CONTENTS

JALOUSIE

Along the Grain

What a figure does to a landscape
head downcast, oblique

You're what's there
to catch the breaking wave

The facts to reconcile

I press into or against
but it's clear:

skin L E A K S
the world comes I N

Debts, textures
some fog in the air

One renders what is happening
moves to say what has been

A tenderness to walk the fault lines
and slip oneself in

In Medias Res

with two fingers mother
lifted my chin

cleaned from my face
the last of the blood

nosebleeds a chore
I was learning

to tend on my own

I learned
the word *prone*

two fingers
light pressure

tilted my face
up to the sky

smeared my lips
in Vaseline

I shut my eyes
to receive

not quite so much sun

eyelids' pink and
flickering wash

I liked it more
than ocean or buildings

or everything passing
sideways outside

what I wanted to know
was what do the blind see

is it static
is it what I see

when I imagine *nothing*
sometimes white space

otherwise black

at the center of the bridge
high ridge and contour

of the land
past the banks

my father
without fail:

imagine sailing onto this

Lenape hills

1609, Henry Hudson
on the *Halve Maen*

vision opens
out, out

then Manhattan
the car subsumed

a knife of sky
no horizon

that was childhood, then childhood was over

one image gone from the skyline

there was the war

we put our bodies in the street

a few hours, a few times a year

then we stopped

block by block the walkups

gone from Yorkville

the idea of home

without purchase

on the feeling

crossing each day
the river

(not a true river
it runs back and forth)

I stare into the fact of others

just the fact

lights turn on
in a room across the street

and someone
visible inside

standing on the roof
my face

and the face
of the buildings

I say my city my gaze

no the body the city
the face with its eyes

under the bald sun
they pass through one another

not a horse through a field

but weather
in an afternoon

the condition of place
inside a body

city a barrage
of surfaces

dark, illumed

in the screen of my phone
my chin reflected

I spoke

American English
was a woman

paid in dollars

forces continuous
around me

as space is
as air

where *to see*
is to have at a distance

what populates vision

things made
and not yet remains

I touch my phone
not sheets of plastic and cadmium

I touch the screen
not copper threads

where vision began
and ended was medias res

at night the trash
I left on the curb

sunrise the sound
of a truck

idling downstairs

(pink and flickering
wash of eyelids

hello blood
inside the face)

a crushing sound
in the hopper

and then it goes

two fingers
I touch my phone

hello mother
hello

I Dreamed a Word That Meant a Break in the Weaving

I dreamed the word for a splinter between weft and warp

It came from Old German

I saw it in the frame

of the pre-loaded dictionary

an ß broke in in the middle

The dream went no further

than the bounds of the window

which bore a faint gingham check

as in a screen seen through a lens

Wherever there's a surface

a quarry, a gash

How to address

the thing at which one is looking

as across the centuries

text takes you in

When Tilted through Waking, Eyes Still Bleary and Slow

In English the burning city
Hecuba dreams in my hand

Come man with cup
and hard-luck pitch

Upstream the brunch rush
shines upon our heads

I take in text
like water into bread

Small change across a counter
the marble top fake

which makes it no less real
no more, no less made

Decade

From the authority
of a bird's eye

likeness lays a second surface
on a river dense with leaves

Photos drift from their deltas

English casts my vision
left to right

In a patchy field
a man kneels down

pours water
from one vessel to another

Grasses trail their fingers
an alphabet works through you

You draw a straight line

And Follow It

The figure having entered
elsewhere, beforehand

flowering symbols
in haze above the sea

All the effort
to lug your small life

as specters of a future
wave about helplessly

Distance draws a mark
vision takes aim

And nigh the water
old friends were moving

by the glow
of the ungraspable

Self-Monument

Let the movie of my life be episodic, arcless.

All the dressing and undressing stitched together,

All walking, all paying

and receiving change.

In one sense, my life's work is dishes.

It's nothing to do with gender.

There is a beginning, middle, and end

to the washing. To letting dry.

The hands go red.

Prepare my eyes for the end of seeing

with fly ash and soot.

Black spit, on the one hand, a symbol.

On the other, men and their lungs.

Promenade

It is spring why not
place your hands
on your sun
-warmed hair
a swell of ease
you can ride
and crossing
your path
is a woman
in low-slung mules
you want
what she has
easy limbs and
deft gait
but don't you
already have it?
the wash
of grasping
a go-to
trick light
in the distance
the latest
new tower o god
to see your hand
rip the sky
and work the glass
the owners
at climax ejected
up to the clouds
the sun

on your chest
the sudden
urge to shop
spilt rice
in the gutter
you think at first
bird guts?
the early day
angled down
in lavish display

Overlay

The workday I am in it

A garment floating in water

That lip of the lake where scum . . .

Hello to the porous hour

where tube light crackles

in pyramidal mount

To each his own ongoingness

To each his own fritz

A body takes particular space

as I sit in the stream

tasked to be not smoothed

Give me all your kings

Give me

by attrition

This Was to Be

This was to be a poem about leisure

About postures of diversion and those of a person at work

From the couch I was watching *Blow Up*

A film, for me, principally about white jeans slashing green expanses
of lawn

In one hand I had Krasdale Puffed Rice with Real Cocoa

An embarrassing purchase

But to admit it does not make me vulnerable

I work for a university

At this time of year we're invited to gatherings with huge amounts of cheese

The abundance I think is not a guess at how much will be consumed but

An investment against the look of a platter mostly eaten

With my fingers on a sliver of comté I think

What I touch has been inside the body of a cow

and now in this carpeted room

(milk being quotation from grass)

are pastures of the Jura

It's the labor of those who pay tuition

that spreads their verdure within me

In my poem about leisure, I remember a Lucy Ives poem that begins

To all other things what I prefer most is thinking what I really think

When at work, I feel I am excused

from needing a personality

I come and go

While time remains neutral, remains indifferent

My boss can't tolerate *Play as It Lays* because the characters, she says, have no *inner life*

A savor of poolside and tears is all I've retained

Forgetting is de facto a kind of refusal

but regarding my own involvement, no sentence

waves the banner of my heart

like Bartleby's *I would prefer not to*

Without his rigorous abstention, that is, without opting de facto to die

it is a stance through which I wink at my stance

an emblem on a tote

that holds my gym shoes and lunch

In the locker room two ladies discuss someone named Barb

who has said to drink iced coffee while working out is *not the worst*

From the shower I hear one say to the other

When someone tells me something I want to do

I believe it

Premise

Having woken from the dream of riding on a flat tire

Having carried the *scrape and-a-one-two, scrape and-a, scrape scrape* onto the train

Having surfaced in a heart of commerce, closed

Having taxed the muscles in a pack of women

Having paid to

Having creamed our faces in a crowded mirror

Having walked a mall-like stretch of a famous avenue

Having passed two men caked in dust, one

Having aimed a miniature leaf blower at his chest

Having turned it on his companion, who

Having swept his arms dramatically

Having pushed the tool gently away, both men

Having laughed, somewhat cleaner

Having caught my reflection in the windowed façade of a bank

Having admired the ranunculus in a garden box of a white-brick building one block long

Having held a low opinion of this architectural style, but that vision of modernity

Having become passé

Having caught a kind of charm in it

Having blushed at nostalgia's dim revision

Having turned left at the park

Having been too early for students, their habitual swarm

Having drawn the emptiness across honeycomb pavement into suspense, the site

Having served as parade ground, public grave, northeastern edge of 19th-century Little Africa, a neighborhood

Having grown from a 17th-century enclave of freemen, despite

Having been stripped of their deeds to the land under British rule, the farm plots

Having been parceled out by the Dutch West India Company to eleven men, who

Having been enslaved by the charter, petitioned for freedom and

Having attained a conditional version, the terms

Having not extended to any children living or future

Having required annual payments of grain and livestock and occasional service, the charter

Having established a plantation to cultivate tobacco, the land

Having formed in a time of resistance a border between settlers to the south and Lenape to the North, the path to Kintecoying

Having followed a stream rich in trout, the water

Having coursed across these eras and—polluted, converted into a sewer, and finally buried—possibly courses

Having nodded good morning to a woman's request for a dollar like I don't understand the ask

Having pulled the heavy institutional door

Having flashed ID to George

Having ridden the elevator to eight

Having forgotten already—one man's shirt was neon orange, but was the leaf blower's matching or green?

Having gone to the desk and turned on the Dell

Having eaten a yogurt purchased on the famous avenue for $1.79

Having gone to the kitchen to recycle the cup, despite

Having seen the bins emptied into a common dumpster

Having nodded to the assorted labors, human and bovine, past and to come

Having said internally *bon voyage*

Having read that plastics remain 450 to 1000 years intact

Having greeted a coworker *Good morning, Good morning*

Having typed *1569* into the browser's search bar

Having wanted 450 years to feel real or specific

Having read Wikipedia's list of deaths in that year, Pieter Bruegel the Elder

Having been among the names

Having turned to the tasks that constitute my employment, e.g.

Having volleyed a quantity of emails

Having projected into that near-future space where *I hope this finds you well*

Having chanted internally from Alice Notley, *All day you have to in the lough*

Having read the line on the morning train

Having said it alternately *law* and *loff*

Having consulted circa 1:00 p.m. Merriam Webster

Having thought, *But in a lake, I never feel that I "have to"*

Having retrieved lunch from the fridge

Having emptied the container onto a plate

Having spoken with coworkers: media, food

Having listened partly while replaying internally the dust exchange

Having cast both shirts as orange

Having recalled *in your orange shirt you look like a better happier St. Sebastian* despite

Having pictured the shirt in the poem not florescent like the tulips O'Hara goes on to mention but something more like sherbet, the men this morning

Having cleaned via pantomime of cleaning

Having slid tenderness inside a macho exchange

Having rendered the image of a rough touch via a light one

Having returned to my desk

Having typed *wedding dance* into the browser

Having encountered a field of photographs showing white people in formal dress move over lustrous floors

Having realized my mistake

Having added *bruegel*

Having seen this painting at the DIA

Having been in town for a wedding

Having gravitated to the reds, the reveling peasants

Having been painted happy and plump, Antwerp

Having operated refineries for the quantities of sugarcane imported from the Americas, the city

Having become rich, Flemish merchants presumably

Having wanted to admire a cheerful image of their commoner countrymen, their carousing

Having been read as a celebration of local customs at a time of Spanish rule but

Having also been read as a moral statement against the underclasses, Flanders

Having been in the throes of the Reformation, on the brink of the Eighty Years' War

Having typed an associative list:

16th c
- "Exploration," e.g.
    - innovations in ship building, cartography
    - transatlantic trade inc. mass enslavement, potatoes in Europe, smallpox in the "new world"
- Calvin / Huguenots / Protestants / print
- Mannerism, Northern Renaissance, secular and daily in visual art
- Marlowe, Spenser, Early Shakespeare, Sidney, Rabelais
- Suleiman the Magnificent, Philip II, Túpac Amaru, Henry VIII, Elizabeth I
- Heliocentrism / Copernicus
- Clocks w multiple hands

Having rendered foremost a picture of an education, the present

Having ground a myopic lens

Having looked through or only at it?

Having opened *Margaret & Dusty* to renew my chant

Having found *all day, hove to,* not *have to; you* nowhere to be found

Having glanced to the corner of the screen: 1:37—*better get back,* but first

Having typed into the search bar *1019*

Having recognized only names: *Song Dynasty, Kyūshū, Manchuria, Kiev,* the year's Wikipedia entry

Having been less than half the length of 1569's—gross distance or the contributors' skew toward Europe (then "dark")?

Having tried too the Met's digital collection

Having turned up photos of ceramic fragments

Having saved a screenshot: *Glaze Clump, 11th–12th century, no image available, not on view*

Having felt a personal affinity

Having scrolled chronologically, the object dated closest to 1019 a single gold dinar *(A.H. 419, A.D. 1028, made in Iran (modern Afghanistan), bequest of Joseph H. Durkee, New York, 1898)*, the coin

Having one smoothed and slightly cracked edge, the details

Having been effaced, perhaps

Having sat unevenly under heat or weight or water

Having felt the air in the office suddenly thicker, the skies

Having opened, I was certain, despite

Having been nowhere near a window

Having thought *the rage of the gods* despite

Having not once considered divine emotion as

Having shaped the observable world

Having inherited instead a humanism in which there are natural forces and people who act and

Having felt that view *scrape and-a scrape,* metal rims

Having bent against road

Regarding the Statues of Great Men

In the sun
their heads become

unendurable
to the touch

Life Among the Monuments

I had come to a meet a friend in a public square
stonework, trees
partitioned the space from heavily trafficked roads
at its center a decorative fountain
whose two-part being
shot water in exuberant plumes
ribald plashing on Neptune's cheek
then dry all winter
my friend approached
and calling out
gave to my form
among the clustered others
a familiar tone
into my hand
my friend placed their gift
white paper cup   white plastic lid
and on dedicated benches
splintered wood and silvery plaques
we mixed our voices
events, feelings
what it was like
little incursions into our separateness
the vast uneasy fact of one
who brushes against
edges into
the ongoing particular
closing our eyes to the good sun
taking in thru our lips

WATER FROM THE NORTH
thru
FRUIT FROM THE SOUTH
in
PAPER FROM THE EAST
thru
POLYPROPYLENE FROM BENEATH THE EARTH
via
TOIL FROM THE TEN DIRECTIONS

to carry in our bloodstreams and submit the rest

MMXX

to fill

Lump Grammar (Theory of Trash)

Inside the unrulable heap
thing abuts thing
the sentence pulled
from geologic distance
through greased lips and ton
gue   thing after
thing never finished
iterative and articulated back
foregone won't finish
whiplash witness like
cartoon head
follows with eyes drawn
mute material fact
through civilizational rock stratum
metal glass
stomach lining carries
plastic thingtime
cold monumental brushed tender
beeswax lips going slack
predicate *had to have been*
because *is*
drip dripping
the potable water
scrawled through
winter-cracked lips
heap of half-life the sentence cannot finish
running into away from and out
a thicket dense and various
each part actual only ever for example
in tombtime belching hole time

eating qualities spitting out
the rumpled after
so as not to say
the imponderably large
illegible list
in relational tangle

Love Poem

I button your shirt and the thought that you are another

with a chest I cannot

inhabit

the placket on the left is where the buttons are sewn

so it's easy

to face

and dress you

day after day you dress yourself of course when I do

it's to pantomime devotion

(itself an act of devotion)

in a world where clothes nod to a world

where a man is dressed and buttoning

is work

for a woman

to do on a man

and from this shirt

and all shirts and things I have bought I know mystery

is alive

like someone's

idea of god

even the single button how to think of it

its roundness or the holes

swirl of color

to make the plastic look like horn

I've been given the idea

of machinery and material and human work—nothing

specific as the fact

of this one shirt (it is here and present) on your body the body I touch

and live beside

like any god this binds me

to the knowledge that my knowledge is made incomplete

I am wrong

when I think my love

could lift you your body or mine like a single stone

from all that gives shape

and weight

to days where light

brings clear empty space

to walk through

Sleeps of Bronze

and into a wide, low basin
        head to fill with water and cotton
ropes to tow the eyes

flowers, the classics
        their blooms in drift, this
most regular horse and rider

        the wind the petals and the clomp clomp clomp

here, at the ledge
waves to float and to wash
        light skimming
on broad, flat hours

and who beyond
this wooly pass (my eye
my tongue of lead)

who
in the sticky tangled wood

        or the hours move by combing,
that is,
I am raked
am straightened

to split my private sleep
into the open dark

    into the densely peopled

imperfectly traversable room

Saturday

When I live on bread and cream and dick and wash my skin with honey

Read in the park where gardeners set out a box of bees

and from my page the sun pulls threads in silver, purple, green

up through a chunk of watermelon

which bleeds in the protagonist's fingers

She's sweating in high summer, coaxing a boy to eat from her hands

He runs off, I get up to walk

past the public court and standing water where I look for the image of the hoop

past the wall, notionally beige but overpainted in strata

so the player smacks his pink Sky Bounce against a giant slice of Napoleon

Past the narrow window with the cardboard SKYLIGHTS sign

then black Mercedes wearing the boot

under a bird who's calling *Don't care don't care don't*

In Public

Night grows a long finger

with which to stir you

Meet friends at a bar

Buy a drink

Another

At the corner

a man plays saxophone in a rubber mask

A body has to

stand for *something*

Run for the bus

and on *WHOSE STREETS*

have I skinned

both knees

Two Street Trees

To have lost the argument's thread:

Events empty into their qualities,
just -*nesses*, residual in me, clot.

I walk under a late-blooming locust
into ambient grape soda—

a likeness such that the palate unacquainted with artificial fruit
could not grasp the real tree's bouquet.

It's June. I'm in love with the reeking world.

Though I know that I am in it,
alone and with others,

I walk a thin space
cleared by doubt, counter doubt.

My questions baled,

my few important things
knock together at the bottom of a tote.

I walk into October and wonder if by living

I have come to grasp negative dialectics
in a realm outside of thought.

One yellow branch cuts the green ginkgo,
of itself and not.

Verisimilitude

Celadon curtains part in a third-floor window. Ground level, someone backs an enormous orchid through the door, in blooms her face obscured.

Penny tossed into the fountain of a developing scene: curtains parted: *pour le passé composé l'action est precise et achevée.*

The walkup wears a crown of pigeons on bird-deterring spikes. Two lift off, the door shuts, exit flower-headed figure.

I, across the Ave, face beige brick, nine windows blinded but the center one, where faint-green fabric drew an inverted V.

The triangle implies depth in soft black, a room where in late-winter light a stranger's—my neighbor's—afternoon is passing.

Even more than her rectangles of sea and sky, Vija Celmins's depictions, in dizzying precision, of paper

move through likeness to the extravisual, where looking wants for touch to know handlings' specters (puckers, creases) as marks on an unbroken plane.

Sentences go single file through action's everywhere vectors, a problem I have with time.

Where white blossoms went on torso and legs, a dusk-to-dawn bulb wraps the street around its surge.

We Like to Say What Is Happening

The finger for beheading

across your phone

Across the facts

one is supposed to reconcile

you take in text

and the day takes you in like a pool

Helicopter drags its shadow

a double surface through the streets

The upshot of a body

is I D I S P L A C E

The air itself

something other than indifferent

when I was walking making little circles with my fingers

to feel the space

out past the skin

Replica

Compelled to admire the manicured gardens of pathological control,
I go narrowly, on a wet day, clutching a pet disdain
and in my hands an umbrella, a good one, although unstylish,
a double balm, as a gift and for its lawns of *Central Park in Spring*
aglow on polyester. From watercolor grass rise boulders,
among them, a rock I named in childhood (for a glacial ridge
and a dense spot of mica) The Golden-Eyed Dinosaur.
Today I woke my worst, wanting nothing but blamelessness,
the coward's lonely itch. If I must be, I'd choose poolside repose,
strung evenly over an hour, concrete and bromine, ice against glass,
but I'd settle for the feminized space of a nail salon, rich, too,
in fumes and pleasant boredom, and someone who holds my fingers.
You can pay for that, not even much. No one will ask me to account
for comfort wrested from labor or the pull toward self-decoration,
but the fact pervades with the stingy sun seeping through my scrim
in green. In language rinsed of god, mercy. On the sidewalk before me,
three trench-coated figures; two bow their plastic rain-bonneted heads.
Without analogy, the statuary I join them at the corner to compose.

Effigy

From my mother's body, a stranger's hands
lifted me, yes,

into the state.

I assembled a vocabulary.
Grew breasts. Moved calendrically

through empty time.

In the junkyard, I unearthed
a cash register and pried

its busted case. I reached in
and lifted the interior.

In my hands, the levers like ribs.

Home, I lather and rinse
the moving parts

so they smell of well-kept men,
the chemical idea of pine.

Any object is a statue-machine,
shapes pointing to bodies.

They charge the space by making me
target and weapon.

Episode in the Life of Saint Hortus
(Conversation on the Psychedelic Lawn)

After Taeyoon Choi

The gods turn up the sun, make it huge, hot-pink
    in the black-hatched sky. Hortus, scrawny sprite,
        appears thrice on ascent through the ornamental trees:
    sitting now on a bough, now swinging, now perched
up top for a word: "O, Sun, I climb toward you
    from the golden below to wash in the leaves your light
most haunts and go a little spectral in devotion. I no longer
    know, does the garden rise in health or radiation? See
the hornbeam trees' Singaporean heights, how
    lately their shadows turn color, get up, and roam.
        Moreover, my friend—see there? down on the ground?—
sprouted fawn legs and can't but sweetly recline…"
The sun's twin heads come out to lay their flesh
    ever so gently over the sky. One draws a solid wind,
        slides Hortus (not by choice) to the grass in safety,
    one gives a light so bright it makes all the world
see-through. In chorus: "Glow contingent, Hortus.
    Leak. Peer into anything—stone, your friend, the air—
        each overlays another. Like so, I drape my hand."

Score for the New Cotillion

do the knees	of the brother	in a stranger's	home video
when he chases	the dog	pulls	the dog's ears
do the left wrist	of an anchor	right arm	of a riot cop
the scalp	of the crowd	*c'mon*	do the pelvis
of the talent	in a blue movie	tilting always	away
add the torso	of a man	in a clip	from a prank
do the second	just before	he eats pavement	*you know*
you're twisty	*little girl*	now switch	it's your neck
after the neck	of the brother	your shins	after the shins
of an anchor	your navel	of the police	and thighs
of the crowd	you've got	the elbows	of the talent
and your lips	*c'mon*	do the lips	of the person falling

In the Next Room

You will find me lying down,
oranges strewn across the floor.
Each day, time pulled me
through work,
autobiography, the nation.
Each space I entered
instructed my posture,
made me a new sculpture.
This is my dream of the afterlife—
an orange at the base of my neck, sacrum,
under the backs of my knees.
In the next room always,
in half-light, adjacent,
our fear and
everything wastable
I was caught up in wasting.

Strange Damage

After Ishmael Houston Jones's Without Hope

This is a pas de deux for a man
who takes a cinderblock as his partner.
He kisses the brick, sets it on his back.
One shoulder leers at the ground.
When he drops the brick it crumbles
and the dancer breaks his silence.
He names each chunk for a bone.
Names them again for fractures.
When the dancer leaves the stage,
he leaves the brick for his body.
Often my dreams are adagios.
I dance the part of the cinderblock.
When I wake my arms look wrong.
I walk the trash downstairs
and find a plastic bottle at my feet.
If I picture bending down for it,
touching too becomes my skin.
There it goes into the street.

What Made It Good

                     to touch the catalog
and its staged interiors, the furniture

unaffordable, out of reach. To read
the product names, unfamiliar enough

to not connote. Cold that I liked to
stand at the closet with my best silks

grazing my face and picture a woman
pluck the cocoons from boiling water.

That I shaved myself to smell like a man,
to think of my legs

more like a strong neck buttoned into
a clean collar. I held greed to my breast

in the house of work and I held it
in the house of provisions. Like doors my sternum

opened. I was a sunlit room where I could
set down my voice, leave it behind.

Jalousie

Rocklike in the blinds' bright–dark dyad,
I intervene. Elegiac couplets cross one cheek,
the other tilts from its own cool splotched against sunlit floor.
Six days I've been indoors, wearing this sweatshirt.
I tire of it and wear it inside out.
Would that I could turn my very skin and call on all things
to bear their linings as a second face.
Orpheus in profile; Orpheus in profile the other way.
In a dream I'm clothed in dirt and ether wet by famous tears.
The heroes weep as often as they fight on the Aegean,
where sand is ground by telling. Repetition on geologic scale
spreads a version of the Rockaways under my Achilles,
who sulks then grieves.
Would that there were a third side to flip onto.
I tan, I burn . . . until death, this object lesson in presence.
As a kid, I'd look across a clean cement courtyard
to TVs constellated in the next building's windows—
NewsHour's blue at six, an orchestra tuning.
I want from the shade not jealous guarding but a medium:
A slat beheads my landlord's swan-shaped planting pot,
and I resolve the view, unstriped and entire.

NOTES

"In Medias Res" quotes Susan Howe's "There Are Not Leaves Enough to Crown to Cover to Crown to Cover" ("to see is to have at a distance").

"Decade" and "And Follow It" together refer to the La Monte Young's *Composition 1960 #10 (for Bob Morris)*, the score for which is "Draw a straight line and follow it."

"This Was to Be" quotes Lucy Ives's "[To All Other Things What I Prefer Most Is Thinking What I Really Think]." "I'd prefer not to" is the refrain of Bartleby, the protagonist in Herman Melville's *Bartleby the Scrivener.*

"Premise" misquotes Alice Notley's "As You Like It" ("All day hove to in the lough") and quotes Frank O'Hara's "Having a Coke with You" ("in your orange shirt you look like a better happier St. Sebastian")

"Score for the New Cotillion" misquotes "Twist and Shout."

"Effigy" adapts the first line of Randall Jarrell's "The Death of the Ball Turret Gunner" ("from my mother's sleep I fell into the state") and refers to Walter Benjamin's notion of homogenous, empty time as defined in "Theses on the Philosophy of History."

"In the Next Room" borrows a posture from one of Erwin Wurm's *One Minute Sculptures.*

"Strange Damage" is after *Without Hope* by Ishmael Houston Jones, as performed at The Chocolate Factory by James McGinn in 2008.

ACKNOWLEDGEMENTS

Poems in *Jalousie* first appeared in *Best New Poets; Birdfeast; BOMB; Boston Review; The Brooklyn Rail; Denver Quarterly; Denver Quarterly's F I V E S; Dusie; Everyday Genius; Fence; jubilat; Kenyon Review Online; The Literary Review; No, Dear; Poetry; The Recluse; Salt Hill; Sixth Finch; Touch the Donkey; The Yale Review;* as part of Monster House Press's pamphlets series; and in the chapbooks *Score Poems* (Present Tense Pamphlets/Northwestern University, 2016), and *Five O'clock on the Shore* (above/ground press, 2019). Thank you to the editors.

Written over more than a decade, the poems in *Jalousie* bear the traces of many important friendships. Thanks to Mike Lala for tireless reading and discussion, for all our shared days. To Danniel Schoonebeek, Tyler Weston Jones, Norah Maki, Jamie Fitzpatrick, Jess Lee, Carson Donnelley, Helena Zhang, Natalie Eilbert, Katie Naughton, Soren Stockman, Monica McClure, Eric Nelson, Dolan Morgan, Matthew Zingg, Keely Kinkead, Jonathan Rajewski, Katie Barkel, Molly Miller-Petrie, Laura Duncan, Zoe Barton, and Claudia Lux, with and from whom I learned how to live as a writer. To my fellow students and teachers at NYU's Creative Writing program, especially Jen Levitt, Emily Barton Altman, Marina Read Weiss, Jenny Xie, Alaina Ferris, Hannah Aizenman, Elisa Gonzalez, Virginia McLure, Meghan O'Rourke, Brenda Shaughnessy, Rachel Zucker, Eileen Myles, Deborah Landau, Yusef Komunyakaa, Craig Morgan Teicher, and Joanna Yas. To Ru Puro, Toby Altman, Emily Skillings, Brittany Dennison, Iris McLoughan, June Foley, Alicia Wright, Cass Eddington, Sara Gilmore, George Life, Nina Vega-Westhoff, Rob McLennan, Marwa Helal, Corinne Butta, and Aiden Farrell who helped me to keep seeing this manuscript through. To Alejandro Varela, Lisa Chen, Nobu Aozaki, Zavé Martohardjono, Mike Clemow,

Amina Henry, and George Fkiaras for sharing space and practice. To Bora Kim and Alessandra Gomez at Lower Manhattan Cultural Council. To my early teachers, especially Leslie Satin, Scott Hightower, Sinan Antoon, Steve Hutkins, Marty Sternstein, Keith Meatto, and Laurel Nyboe. To those whose attention and labor made the manuscript into a book: Dianna Khoi Nguyen for selecting it; Kristina Marie Darling, David Rossitter, and Jeffrey Levine for publishing it. To my parents, Sheree Silvey and Philip Paty, for everything.